AF146276

Zensho W. Kopp
True Life Through Zen

This book is the extended version of the audio book which was published by Amazon Publishing under the same name. In their letters to the author, many listeners expressed the wish to have the audio recording in book form so that they may delve more deeply into its profound wisdom. This wish has now led to the text at hand.

Translation © 2017 by John Kitching
Original title: "Wahres Leben aus Zen",
published by EchnAton Verlag 2015

Producer and publisher: Books on Demand GmbH,
Norderstedt

Cover design: Michel Schmidt
Image enhancement: Jörg Zimmermann
Zensho portrait photo: Verena Kopp
Typesetting: Torsten Zander
List of photographers (www.echnaton-verlag.de)

All rights reserved. This book, or parts thereof, may not be reproduced in any form without permission.

Visit our website at www.tao-chan.org
ISBN: 978-3-7347-435-59

Zensho W. Kopp

True Life
Through Zen

Spiritual self-realisation
in daily life

Contents

Tao Chan

The actions and the quietude of those who have mastered Zen are like passing clouds – without ego-consciousness. It is like the full moon – reflected everywhere. Those who have achieved mastery in Zen are not held up by anything; in the midst of all things they still remain free of all things.

Zen Master Hong-zhi (twelfth century)

Preface

We are living in a time in which more and more people are striving to combine a spiritual and active life. They are seeking a contemporary, holistic way of spiritual realisation which they can live in the midst of daily life in our modern world of today.

This unique book does justice to the continually growing urge for a purposeful life. It is very different from the usual publications on this subject, which on the whole are written by western authors who lack a true understanding of the profound truth of Zen.

By contrast, we are dealing in this book with the work of a realised Zen Master of our modern times who writes "directly from the source of Zen", so to speak. Thus, this book takes on a most special value in that it can change our whole life.

Zen Master Zensho's practical instructions for Zen practice in daily life make the book a reliable orientation-aid for the modern western person. True-to-life and with utter clarity he shows us what this Zen practice is all about and how it leads us to inner peace, deeper wisdom and a meaningful life. Contemporary and easily understood, he imparts to us the holistic Zen way, based on his personal experience. It is the way to a heedful life, filled with awareness, so that we are completely free at all times and are one with the various situations of everyday life. In Zensho's words:

> As master of each situation in the midst of all things we continue to remain completely free from all things. Thus we can go beyond all restricting circumstances and can break through to the essence in the midst of worldly situations.

In this way we experience how we can achieve spiritual clarity and joy in ourselves in everyday life, as the true place of practice. Thus we reach greater freedom and become able to experience the preciousness of each moment with our whole being, and live crystal-clear awareness and our active involvement in life as a single reality. This book is benefitted greatly by Zensho's detailed "Introduction to the holistic Zen way", which, with great clarity, provides the reader with a compact summary of the active Zen way in the midst of the world.

A further benefit in this exceptional book are the many quotes of the old Chinese Zen masters, whose mystical sayings often lie completely beyond all possibilities of intellectual understanding.

Nevertheless, Zensho's illuminating explanations provide us with a valuable key to a better understanding. Without these exceedingly helpful explanations from a Zen master who draws from the same enlightened consciousness dimension as the old Chinese Zen masters, the deeper meaning of many of these sayings would remain concealed from us.

Zensho's clear and simple way of teaching, together with his humorous geniality, is a stimulating mix of refreshing humour and earnestness. Thus, in this extremely lively book, which breathes the spirit of Zen, we feel the direct presence and realisation of one of the most significant wisdom teachers of our times. His method of spiritual conveyance is of original directness and is unique and unmistakable in its manner. The book "True Life Through Zen" shows us a way out of the narrowness of our self-made limitations. And if we immerse ourselves completely in its profound wisdom, our lives will be filled with meaning and become richer.

This book shows us that we do not need to search for the happiness we all long for, since it is already present in ourselves here and now as our true being. We need only immerse ourselves in it.

October, 2015   Zen-Center Tao Chan
                                              Wiesbaden

Introduction
to the holistic Zen way

The inexpressible secret of the Eternal

Zen is the way of instantly perceiving reality. It puts aside all philosophical speculation on the inexpressible truth so that it may point directly to the essence, without any circumlocutions.

This essence is the Enlightenment of the mind, and thus liberation from our attachment to the cycle of birth and death. For this reason, Zen is primarily about our awakening to that reality of our true being which neither begins with birth nor ends with death.

This, our true essence, is the underlying reality at the base of all our experiences. As the pure source of all being it is pure being, absolute consciousness and boundless bliss. However, this reality is not something we must seek, for it is constantly present as our absolutely inherent true essence – we have never lost it. It reveals itself "now-here", we need not wait for any other opportunity. Therefore, it is said in Zen:

Where do you wish to seek the ox when you are already sitting on the ox you are seeking?

Following the path of Zen means completely immersing ourselves in this reality of our true being "here and now". Yet what really is the truth of Zen? The Chinese Zen Master Yung-chia (eighth century) answers this question as follows:

Everything I could say of it would fall short of the mark.

In other words, the absolute truth cannot be expressed in words because our human speech is very limited. Therefore, each attempt to describe the profound truth of Zen with our limited speech, regardless of how well-meant it may be, is completely pointless. And the more we are imbued with the fullness of divine essence, the less capable we become of linguistically expressing the inexpressible mystery of the Eternal in words.

Furthermore, each mental image we make of the highest truth is just an idea and a far cry from reality. The more we then cling to this idea, the more it will even become a great obstacle on the path to realisation. For this reason, the Chinese Zen Master Lin-chi (ninth century), one of most significant masters in the history of Zen, says:

If you meet Buddha, then kill him!

Direct perception

If you wish to experience the truth of Zen, you must come into direct contact with it and must not allow yourself to be separated from reality by concepts and notions. For Zen is the path of direct perception. Since this is so, what possibility do we have at all for experiencing the truth of Zen?

Here, the old Chinese Zen masters give us this well-meant piece of advice: "Stop your seeking!" In the words of the Chinese Zen Master Huang-po from the ninth century – one of the colossal figures of Zen:

> If you wish to achieve realisation on the Zen path,
> you need not study any doctrine. You must only
> learn how to avoid seeking and attaching yourselves
> to anything. Where nothing is sought, the unborn
> Mind reveals itself. Where there is no attachment
> the indestructible Mind is present.

With this very well-meant advice, Zen Master Huang-po challenges us to give up our search for the truth and return to the present moment. This means that we turn to our true Self, which reveals itself in all its glory now-here in this instant.

Yet, by identifying with our false self, the ego, our "ego-delusion", we constantly cover the reality of our true being with the dark clouds of our spiritual blindness. In our identification with the erroneous feeling of individuality we simultaneously create the world we experience with all its pain and suffering, and we become more and more entangled in the cycle of birth and death.

In our desire for liberation from this entanglement in suffering, the question arises in us on the meaning of all existence, and we start seeking externally for an answer. Yet seeking externally for the truth, as the reality of our true being, and viewing it as something independent from ourselves equates to the dualistic mentality of wishing to understand things with our intellect. For since we are already living in the midst of this reality and through this reality anyway, we cannot be different from it or separated from it. Our true nature is already consummate right now and has always been so. In Zazen Wasan, the "hymn of praise of Zazen", one of the essential texts in Zen, the Japanese Zen Master Hakuin (eighteenth century) says:

We have been Buddha from the very beginning on. Just as there is no ice without water, there is not one person without Buddha. Although people constantly carry the truth within them, they do not perceive this and seek afar. They suffer from thirst and do not see the well close at hand. They live in poverty and forget that they are heirs to an immeasurable treasure.

You say that you suffer. Yet you only suffer through your ignorance. Awaken from your dream! And the mistakes of the past will no longer torment you. Where is hell? You left it in yesterday's dream.

Where is paradise? You are already in its midst.

We are already in the midst of the all-embracing wholeness of being. Absolute reality is constantly present when we are present. That is why Zen is only interested in what takes place in this instant "now-here". There is no existence beyond this moment, for the past has gone and is no longer, and the future is just a thought.

The present moment of Now

The only reality which exists is "Now". Beyond this, nothing exists. Therefore, the only possibility for us to experience our true being is when we immerse ourselves completely in the present moment.

If we are completely present – truly here – then everything is here! In this state of pure awareness we experience our own essence with such intensity and inner joy that our whole life changes. Then we will experience the marvel of life within ourselves and beyond ourselves, everywhere and at all times, for the mystery of being lies within ourselves. Everything flows from our own heart.

In this instant – right here where we are – the fullness of divine being reveals itself, now-here, as the truth of Zen. It is not a goal to be reached at some point in time but a pure matter of recognising. For since absolute reality is the all-embracing wholeness of being, it encompasses boundless space and the three time-forms: past, present and future in a single "Now". Here, everything falls into one single point. By experiencing the direct, absolute presence of Now, we experience the multidimensionality of the boundless reality of the One Mind. In the words of the Chinese Zen Master Yuan-wu (twelfth century):

> When a grain of dust is raised, it contains the entire earth. When a flower blossoms, the whole world leaps forth.

In the moment-consciousness of Now, we enter into the space- and timelessness of pure being, and we recognise that the present moment is eternal. For Now has no before and no afterwards – thus it is eternity itself as beginningless and endless pure being. However, the experience of space-time is nothing other than the result of the conditioned, perceiving consciousness, and thus illusion.

Past, present and future are nothing more than thoughts which appear in the mind at the present moment and which take on the form of a whole universe. Everything is simply the game of the natural creativity of the mind, in which and through which all things appear like in a dream.

The experience of an external world of phenomena in space and time is therefore nothing other than thinking. But Zen says, "all thinking is an erroneous opinion". From this we must conclude: space and time do not exist. This means that our entrapment in the cycle of birth and death is nothing more than a delusion – a dream without any reality.

The way of Zen is for us to break through this deceptive nature of all phenomena by achieving transcendental wisdom and awakening to the reality of the One Mind, which is beyond space and time. In this awakening we experience the great Liberation. The light of the One Mind shines forth and in an instant we experience that everything is just the way it is – Tathata, the thus-is reality of the One Mind.

This One Mind, beside which nothing else exists, is our original essence and the source of all joy. For there is no greater joy than in recognising our true self. It is our true being, which neither begins with our birth nor ends with our death and reveals itself as reality "here-now".

In this consciousness of non-discriminating clarity of mind we experience ourselves as One with all beings and feel reverence and all-embracing love for all that exists. Once we have experienced this pure awareness, many things which were important to us in life lose their meaning and fall away. For we recognise their unreality and meaninglessness, such that our motivation for them dissolves and our dreams crumble away.

The illusion of time

Only the One Mind is real, space and time have no true existence. They are only mental conditions with which the individual consciousness perceives a supposed, external world in space and time. Yet being free from the illusion of time means being free from the mistake of taking your identity from the interwoven memories of your dead past. Being free from the illusion of time also means that we do not project our desire for fulfilment into the future. For if we are only focussing our sights on the future, in the constant hope that better circumstances will arrive which will change our lives, we are missing out on true life.

In our obsessive desire to arrive somewhere and achieve something, we cannot perceive true life which reveals itself now-here in its full beauty. Spiritually blind and deaf for reality, we are unable to experience the marvel of life which unfolds everywhere around us in its entire fullness. Thoughtlessly living away in this state of indifferent non-awareness, in the delusion of space and

time and in mindless routine means "being spiritually dead". In today's world, most people are constantly on the run from the present, driven by their autonomous habitudinal-energy of wishing to achieve something.

Inwardly they are filled with restlessness, driven by the autonomous projection mechanisms of their discriminating thinking and wishing. They are constantly in a hurry, so that they can no longer stop, and thus they miss out on true life.

In their desire for status, success and security in life they sacrifice their health to earn plentiful money. Then they sacrifice their money in order to regain their health. The whole time they are so filled with worries and fears about their uncertain future that they cannot enjoy the living present. They live as though they would never die, and then they die without having ever really lived.

However, the present moment of absolute Now is true life, which reveals itself now-here in its complete fullness. Therefore, on the Zen way it is essential that we completely immerse ourselves in this reality here and now, in crystal-clear self-awareness of mind. Everywhere, wherever we may be, at all times and in all that we do.

Zen in everyday life

Pay full attention to each activity of daily life, then each instant will become an intensive experience. For our life has only so much meaning and depth as we have awareness. Only in the light of pure consciousness does everything become meaningful and precious.

In this way we transcend the everyday world, without alienating ourselves from it or rejecting it in any way. Thus, we retain our inner stability even in the midst of particularly distracting external circumstances in everyday life, and in all daily activities, without losing our spiritual awareness. Then we experience that our true self is present in the midst of our daily lives as the "everyday mind". This consciousness of the everyday mind is the true Zen mind. That is why the Chinese Zen Master Nansen (eighth century) says:

> The everyday mind is the true way. When you achieve the way, your mind becomes as vast and as open as the sky, free of all limitations and boundaries.

In this crystal-clear consciousness of non-discriminating clarity we retain our absolute independence, and remain in accordance with wherever we happen to be and whatever we are currently doing.

We do not allow external circumstances to tear us away and we do not permit ourselves to be drawn into the samsaric confusions and spiritual blindness of an average earth-bound person. We are completely free to come and go as we see please, for we are beyond all dualistic discrimination. This is "True life through Zen". Living in the midst of the world and at the same time being free from the world is the original, vivacious Zen way. Zen Master Hong-zhi (twelfth century) tells us this too:

> When the perception of objects does not blind you, you see that all things are the light of the mind. With every step you surpass everything, completely free, stopping nowhere. With great clarity and unforced, open awareness you unfold in the world.

Here, we live the profound truth of Zen. It is constantly present and is found in the most ordinary things of everyday life. The mystery and wonder of Zen reveals itself to us in drinking a cup of tea or peeling an apple. An old Zen saying puts it as follows:

Miraculous deeds and acts full of wonder! I draw water and carry firewood.

Zen-consciousness is a pure, crystal-clear state of mind in which only the immediacy of the present moment exists and nothing else. However, this can only be experienced by those who behold things from out of the present moment. Therefore, it is said in Zen: "Embrace the moment and be truly here now!" In the words of Zen Master Ma-tsu (eighth century):

In the awareness of this original, pure mind, you act spontaneously and naturally when dressing, eating and in all that you do your whole life long, taking things just as they arise, and thus you unfold your spiritual nature.

By attaining this consciousness, free from all discriminating thinking, we become open for the experience of our true essence, which lies beyond all understanding. When the mind frees itself this way from its self-made limitations, liberation is to be found everywhere. For "Zen is a life without chains, a life in freedom and is freedom itself". And so, break the self-made chains of the grasping, little ego, and the true self radiates in its entire magnificence – all-encompassing and all pervading! Our original, true being is completely free and without the slightest discrimination or contrariness. It is the omnipresent, pure, radiating nature of being and manifests itself as mysterious, peaceful joy.

In this consciousness of wonderful clarity, all duality of subject and object has completely vanished. As a result, all existence and all beings reveal themselves as our true self, which pervades the whole universe.

Through this liberating true life through Zen we are in absolute oneness with the supramundane, and likewise we encompass the whole realm of the all-embracing wholeness of being.

Summer 2015   Zensho W. Kopp
Wiesbaden

1

The True
Path of Zen

The wonderful promise

The radiating light of the One Mind – the reality of our true Being – is always present. Yet this, our original essence, is constantly covered by the dark clouds of our deep-rooted thought-habits and behaviour patterns. For this reason we are unable to perceive our true essence and wander lost in the cycle of birth and death.

The Chinese Zen Master Huang-po from the ninth century clearly describes to us how we can liberate ourselves from this deceptive process of our self-made veil of illusion:

> The One Mind, the source of all things, shines eternally in the blaze of its own perfection. If you would finally throw off all conceptual thought in a flash, the One Mind as your True Being would manifest itself like the sun ascending through the void and illuminating the whole universe without hindrance or bounds.

What a wonderful promise the words of Zen Master

Huang-po indeed hold. Yet what can we do and what is the way we must take to experience our true reality constantly and everywhere? This way to experiencing our original, being is, in terms of Zen, nothing other than "the everyday mind".

This is the astoundingly sobering answer also given by the Chinese Zen Master Nansen in the eighth century to a Zen monk who comes to him and asks:

"What is the true way of Zen?"
And Master Nansen answers:
"The everyday mind is the true way."

In other words: The reality of our true, Divine Being, which underlies everything, is all-pervading. It reveals itself everywhere and at all times and thus in the "midst" of even the commonest of activities. Therefore, we do not need to retreat from the world in the hope of achieving realisation in quiescent woodland solitude or in a monastery.

True-to-life Zen practice

Especially today, more and more people are seeking a spiritual way which is free from religious dogmas and convoluted philosophies. They are seeking a holistic way which they can practise in daily life. Vivacious, original Zen, as it was lived and taught by the old Chinese Zen masters, does this need justice. For it is the spiritual path we can practise in the bustle of everyday life as the true place of practice and also whilst fulfilling our daily duties. It is a very powerful and true-to-life practice which rises

above every form of discrimination. And since non-discrimination is a major element in Zen, a true man of Zen will see no sense in withdrawing himself for the rest of his life in a monastery in order to renounce the world.

Instead, he will realise that he must achieve a non-discriminating clarity of mind within the multitudinous world of duality. That is true Zen practice: to follow the path to liberation in the midst of a world of greed, rejection and spiritual blindness. In the words of the Chinese Zen Master Yuan-wu from the twelfth century:

You need not give up activity in the world in order to achieve effortless awareness of mind. You must know that worldly activity and effortless awareness are not two disparate things – only by thinking of rejecting or grasping do you make two out of them.

But when you can attune yourself to changing circumstances in the bustle of everyday life and can act accordingly; at the same time remaining inwardly empty and calm, then you are vivacious, wherever you may be. For only he who has achieved the essence can be internally empty and in accordance with the external.

2

Acting in accordance with Tao

Intentionless self-awareness

Zen is the path beyond all discrimination since it is free like the birds in the sky and the fish in the sea. Yet life is full of situations in which it is necessary to think, differentiate and act specifically. Then we must carefully consider what the correct decision and accordingly, what the correct method of action should be. Here, it is very important that we retain a non-projecting, non-discriminating clarity of mind. We do this by achieving a self-awareness which is free from intentions.

From this non-identifying, clear viewpoint we can see things undistortedly, just as they are. Then, when we act, we remain in this awareness of mind and in harmonic unison with heaven and earth.

The true nature of our mind is pure, radiant self-awareness. However, self-awareness is not a function of our perception but "pure perception itself". When we achieve this crystal clear consciousness, our whole being will be transformed. In all our activities we will have the wonderful feeling of standing above these activities. Then whatever we do, it will no longer be what it once was, but instead will have a completely new quality. By realising this state of mind of crystal clear consciousness we come naturally to an unswerving serenity. Thus all our actions take place directly and immediately, with gut instinct, so that we remain detached and natural in all that we do – wherever we may be.

Therefore, it is very important that we achieve this empty, clear awareness of mind so that we are intensely conscious at all times and truly immerse ourselves in life – that is to say – in Beingness. For Zen means: "Immersing oneself in the reality of Being". However, immersing ourselves in here and now does not mean having more quantity, by believing we must experience as much as possible. Rather, in terms of Zen it means: "Being open to the all-embracing wholeness of Being". In the words of Zen Master Nansen: "Be as vast and open as the heavens and you are in Tao", and thus we are in the plenitude of Divine Being, right here.

In this respect, "non-intentionality" is the fundamental, essential term for the whole of Zen practice. It pertains to non-identifying action which is free from all ego-induced attachment. It is that attitude of mind which, as the basic principle of the Chinese teachings on Taoism, is expressed by the word "Wu-wei". Wu-wei means "non-action". In terms of Zen and Taoism this non-action is never passive inactivity in which one just sits there and does nothing. Instead, true Wu-wei means that we are in harmonic unison with the all-embracing wholeness of being. Thus, our actions become placid acting "without an actor" so that we act without having the feeling of being the one who acts.

Victory without a sword

One must view Wu-wei as a state of mind whose effect is of the highest grade, and from which any action is possible at any time. The following story is a very good illustration of this state of mind, shaped by Taoism:

The renowned Japanese sword master Bokuden from the fifteenth century was once challenged to a fight by a hot-tempered, half-drunken samurai during a boat trip.

The old master retorted that his mastery in sword fighting no longer consisted of gaining victory over others with the sword but of winning "without" drawing the sword.

However, the half-drunken samurai stubbornly insisted on his challenge. He shouted at Bokuden in rage that he should not talk such rubbish and should instead draw his sword and fight with him. Bokuden recognised that the raging samurai could not be dissuaded from his intention and therefore proposed that if it really must be, the duel could take place on a small, nearby island so as not to endanger the other passengers. After a while the samurai reluctantly agreed and waited impatiently for the great moment of the duel. When the boat reached the island the hot-tempered samurai made an enormous leap onto land and with a great war cry he drew his sword.

At the same moment, however, Bokuden took the rudder out of the boatman's hand with lightning speed and pushed the boat back out into the lake. "That is what you call victory 'without' a sword!" he called back to the

stunned samurai he had left behind. Here, the Taoist attitude of mind of Wu-wei, in the sense of non-action, comes wonderfully into its own as noncombat. It would have been very easy for Bokuden to play off his combative predominance in sword fighting against the samurai. Yet the old sword master Bokuden prevails over the pugnacious samurai in a wonderful way, without even having to draw his sword. The old Taoist Master Lao-tse, the great father of Taoism from the sixth century B.C. calls this:

> To move forth without moving oneself,
> to ward off without lifting one's arms,
> to throw back without attacking,
> to conquer without taking up arms.
> And so:
> Wherever there is a call to arms,
> he who retreats will always win.

He who retreats wins by letting his opponent's attack pass by him so that it fades to nothing and the attacker himself is overthrown. Therefore, in each situation where action is necessary, we withdraw ourselves during the action such that the universal force of the Tao acts through us, for "Doing non-action, everything is wisely done," says Lao-Tse. This means when we act whilst remaining in non-action it is "correct action in unison with the universal flow of the Tao".

3

The omnipresence of Tao

Zen in the midst of the world

If we wish to be in unison with the wholeness of being, we cannot exclude ourselves from the totality. For Tao, the reality of Divine Being, is omnipresent; and contrary to the belief of many esoteric "pseudo-Taoists" of our times it does not only manifest itself in a beautiful countryside where a romantic mountain stream is rushing past.

No! Right in the middle of a noisy fairground and in a beautiful countryside – everywhere, wherever we may be, Tao manifests itself right there. At a main motorway junction during rush hour, when thousands of cars are hurtling past with a great deal of noise, Tao is present right there. Of course it is also to be found in the forest and in tranquillity.

In every form of daily life we encounter the underlying and thus omnipresent Tao; we must only immerse ourselves in it. We need not crave for special moments or places of quietude. For this reason the Chinese Zen Master Hung-Chih says in the twelfth century:

When you grasp the voidness of all things and have achieved this voidness, you are independent of all states of consciousness and completely free in every situation. The original light is ubiquitous and you are in clear, bright accordance with everything, wherever you may be.

It is essential to be inwardly open and adaptable, and outwardly to deal with things without haste. Be like a mirror, which reflects images, and you will rise above all turmoil.

The reality of Divine Being reveals itself to us in all of life's situations. There is nowhere we need look for it. In the words of the Chinese Zen Master Ying-an from the twelfth century:

If you wish to see concealed reality, it is very easy. Be completely present, so that you are in awareness of mind whatever you may be doing, be it eating, walking or speaking, and also in all the demands which the world places on you, regardless of how high they may be.

In the plenitude of Divine Being

Zen is an extremely practical matter and nothing for out-of-touch esoteric dreamers. It puts aside all trifles and speculations on the inexpressible truth so that it may point directly to the essence. For this reason, Zen Master Ta-hui from the twelfth century gives us this good advice:

> Simply free your mind. Do not be too tense nor too lax – this will save you an endless amount of spiritual energy. Just take each situation as it comes and you will be in accordance with everything without any further effort on your part.

We are already "right there", in the plenitude of Divine Being, which pervades the entire universe. It is always there, and we can experience it when our awareness is completely present in Here and Now. Then we abide in the all-embracing wholeness of being.

Yet when we are not present, and instead our thoughts are here and there, we cover the radiating magnificence of the One Mind with the illusion of multiplicity. This multiplicity means dualistic, space-time consciousness – a myriad of thoughts, notions and concepts and thus much discrimination and many problems.

Therefore, when thoughts arise and become autonomous, all notions arise and the feelings associated with them. And when feelings arise, we lose the ability for unconditioned, clear perception and action.

Yet when we become aware of the deceptive nature of all these processes and return to non-intentional awareness of mind – all this overlay we have caused disappears. In that instant, the radiating One Mind, which is constantly present behind this apparent multiplicity as our true being, will reveal itself in its entire magnificence.

4

The way
and the goal
are one

Tao lies under the soles of your feet

One of the most important figures in the history of Zen was the Chinese Zen Master Joshu, who lived in the ninth century and reached the very old age of 119 years. It is said that his words were of such power, that, like a sharp sword, they could instantly cut through the entwinement of his disciples' discriminating, conceptual thought. Here is one of the best known examples:

> During the communal breakfast in the monastery, a monk comes to Zen Master Joshu and says:
> "I am new here at the monastery and want to ask if you would instruct me."
> Joshu asks him, "Have you already had breakfast?"
> The monk replies, "Yes, master."
> And Joshu says, "Good, then go and wash your bowl."
> The monk has the honest wish to experience the truth of Zen and therefore, after the communal breakfast in the monastery, he goes to Joshu and asks him for instruction. But Joshu only answers with: "Go and wash your bowl."

With this unusual answer, the old master hits the nail of the present situation right on the head. The loving compassion of a great buddha radiates from his words. The monk does indeed follow the master's instructions but since he is slow-witted he does not understand what Joshu really means. Therefore, in the language of Zen one must say, "He is sitting on the fairest horse and does not know how to ride it."

The monk wishes to understand the Zen way so that he may attain Enlightenment. Yet Zen says, "The way and the goal are one." The way and the goal are not two things separate from one another. Therefore, it is entirely wrong when you think you can follow the way in the hope and expectation of reaching a goal. That is why Zen says, "If you seek Tao, look beneath the soles of your feet."

The secret of Zen

Following the Way means completely immersing yourself in the reality of Here and Now. For since reality is the all-embracing totality of being, it embraces all three notions of time – past, present and future – in a single "now"! Now, here, everything falls together into one single point. For now, in this instant, beyond all speculative thinking, the whole mystery of Zen reveals itself.

For this reason Zen Master Joshu says, "Go and wash your bowl." In other words, stop standing around uselessly, and do not gabble such rubbish, but rather do what the present situation requires. Do what is necessary and do not needlessly waste your time on insolvable, philosophical problems. Immerse yourself directly in the present moment – and you will experience what the truth of Zen is.

This immersion must be done in such a consequential way that we leave everything behind us, whatever it may be; all behaviour and thought patterns – simply everything. This is far better than building a meaningless discussion on false concepts. Therefore, there is no point in constructing mind-bending speculations and piling up intellectual refuse.

For all speculative, philosophical thought is only of relative value, and ultimately it must be transcended. Whether we read the scriptures of Buddhist philosophy, the Advaita-Vedanta scriptures, or the Buddhist Sutras, they are all but "fingers which point to the moon but not the moon itself", as it is said in Zen. Yet when you are determined to immerse yourself entirely in the truth you must leave all this far behind you. Zen Master Lin-chi from the ninth century gives us this well-meant advice:

You cling to definitions and sayings, and these become obstacles and conceal your perception of the truth. Yet just allow thinking and seeking to come to rest. Turn your attention to that which presents itself to you. Trust in that is acting in you right in this instant, and there is nothing else to seek.

5

Here and now is eternity

The illusion of time

One day, a Zen monk came to Zen Master Joshu and asked him, "Which Zen was once brought from India to China by the first patriarch Bodhidharma?" Joshu answered, "What sense is there in speaking of such an old story? What is 'your' Zen 'now' at this very moment?"

At this instant – right here where you are – the whole truth of Zen reveals itself. We can neither find it in the past nor in the future. Here and Now is eternity itself, and the experience of time is nothing but the result of thinking, it is illusion and thus non-existent.

The old Indian sages used to use one and the same word for the concepts of "time" and "death". In Sanskrit it is called "Kahla". These enlightened Seers had recognised that time and death are the same. Thus, living in the state of indifferent ignorance in the illusion of space and time means being "spiritually dead". For the illusion of time belongs to death. Yet absolute "now" is life – it is eternity. In general we are convinced that time runs in a straight line from the past, through the present, to the future. On this straight time line we live our lives and split it into before and after. But the past has already happened, the present is intangible, and the future does not yet exist.

Past and future are but thoughts which appear in the mind at the present moment. Therefore, the experience of time is nothing more than thought. Yet Zen says, "All thought is an erroneous belief". Only "now" exists and nothing else. Zen Master Huang-po expresses it as follows:

> As soon as thoughts arise you succumb to dualism. Eternity and the present moment are one and the same. There is no beforehand and no afterwards. Only due to your ignorance do you discriminate between these two. Yet, if you would truly understand, how could there still be any discrimination? Understanding this truth is called "perfect, unsurpassed realisation".

Behind all thought, beyond the illusion of space and time, our original, true being before our birth reveals itself. Yet we can only experience this reality of our true being, which is constantly present, if we immerse ourselves completely in "Here and Now". This means: be aware – in crystal clear self-awareness of mind. Be fully consumed by this moment. This is "the direct Zen way to liberation", the Zen way of instantly grasping reality as it is!

The natural state of the mind

Do not be fixated, but rather, stay completely natural and spontaneous during all the demands of daily life. Yet as soon as you think, "I am totally relaxed in here and now," you are captivated yet again and caught in thinking, so that you lose your naturalness. Thus it is important to let the mind dwell in its natural state, for the natural mind is the radiating Dharmakaya – highest reality.

We must not make the mistake either of grasping hold of quietude, such that we find external sounds disturbing. When we hear a sound – we become completely one with the sound. Become the sound of a passing aircraft yourself, become the barking of a dog and the singing of a bird. Whatever it may be it is all One. The perceiver, the process of perception and the perceived are all a single reality.

Everything we perceive is just waves of our own mind and consequently the mind itself. Nothing comes from beyond the mind. It is general belief that our mind assimilates external impressions and experiences, but this is a great misconception! The truth is that the mind encompasses everything. Everything is the deceptive spectacle of the mind. If you believe you perceive something externally it only means that it appears in your consciousness. In an old Buddhist text by the Tibetan Mahamudra Master Orgjenpa from the thirteenth century it is written:

There are no external phenomena which are not mind. Your habitual delusional ideas do not really exist. Everything is completely equal in the mind. True nature is in itself empty and unborn like the boundless heavens.

Phenomena are like reflections. If you take them to be real you will be deceived by the mind's illusions. The world of appearances is the mind's game: if you cling to it you will be deceived by the mind's own phenomena. It is all but an illusory, magical spectacle.

6

Crystal-clear self-awareness

The illusion of multiplicity

The true nature of the mind is pure, radiating self-awareness. Thus, in Zen practice this essentially means attaining an uninterrupted non-intentional self-awareness of the mind. A detached and relaxed attitude of mind is and constantly remains the basic requirement for achieving self awareness of the mind. However, we cannot do this "wilfully". Instead we need only "allow" self-awareness of the mind – as our original, natural state – to happen.

In this effortless awareness, the true nature of our unborn and thus deathless mind manifests itself in the ongoing process of our spiritual realisation. This is "the suchness of reality, beyond birth and death". For there, where eternal reality reveals itself, there is no before and no after. According to the Buddhist teachings this means: In our true being – beyond our delusion of a personality – we are unborn and undying.

Therefore, it is a mistaken assumption held by the conditioned, dualistic mind to believe that we were born and will one day die. Likewise, it is a great mistake to believe that there is a multitude of different beings and things. All these are just reflections which appear in the mind. For everything is just a dream – the illusionary spectacle of the mind, and is devoid of all reality. For this reason the Chinese Zen Master Han-shan says in the seventeenth century:

> Nothing exists beyond the mind. The true Zen student should therefore view all phenomena as clouds passing by in the sky – transitory and unreal like in a dream. Not only the external world but also all habitual thoughts, all passions and desires of our mind are equally without substance and unreal.
>
> Primordially, there is neither body, mind nor world, just as there are no false ideas or emotionally determined thinking. They are all just reflections which appear in the true mind.

Seeing through the deceptions

The reason we cling to phenomena is due to the force of habitual dualistic deception. This causes a multitude of identifications and judgements, through which we are caught in the cycle of conditional existence. The more a person is a prisoner of the illusion of multiplicity, the more he feels himself to be separated from everything. And the more he feels separated in his discriminating perspective of subject and object, the more he feels unsettled and threatened.

Thus the tendency arises in him to defend, shield and protect himself. This can then escalate to extreme

aggression. Yet the real problem here lies solely in the fact that he sees things in a completely wrong way. He has a false mental picture which he projects onto everything and as the result of his spiritual blindness this leads to grasping and rejecting.

Therefore, in Zen practice it is fundamentally important that within this dream of an external world of phenomena in space and time we achieve crystal clear awareness of mind so that more and more, we see through all habitual deceptions. Yet we can only do this when we abide in cheerful serene reflection of the mind, detached and relaxed in all that we do.

Here, "cheerful serene" refers to the tranquillity of non-thinking, achieved through liberation from autonomous compulsive thinking. "Reflection" refers to the lucid self-awareness which reflects everything like a gleaming mirror. Cheerful serene reflection of the mind thus means a "non-intentional, brightly radiating self-awareness in the tranquillity of non-thinking".

Whoever achieves this effortless awareness of the Self-Mind, which lies at the base of everything, no longer entangles himself in the creeping snarl of his own projections. He frees himself from the shackles of discriminating conceptual thinking and the illusion of multiplicity.

He no longer experiences the world from a limited frog-perspective, from which he can just about see to the next tuft of grass, not knowing what lies beyond. Instead he rises far above like the eagle, which from up high, sees everything as a simultaneity. That is "the multidimensional perspective of consummate perceptive clarity", the perspective of non-discrimination.

The Heart-
Meditation
of all Buddhas

7

The self-mind is buddha

Even when clouds cover the moon, the moon is always there, just like the brightly radiating Self-Mind. It is constantly present, even when hidden behind the dark clouds of discriminating, conceptual thinking. Take, for example, the following occurrence:

> The Chinese Zen Master Yun-chu from the ninth century said to a monk, "The Self-Mind is buddha." The monk replied, "Alas I cannot understand that. May I ask you to help me?" The master replied, "In order to help you, let us call him buddha. Turn your consciousness inwards and see yourself what this Self-Mind is."

The path to experiencing this Self-Mind as our true being is to train ourselves in constant, uninterrupted self-awareness of mind – everywhere and at all times, in all that we do. This is also expressed in the "Jewelled Adornment of Liberation", an old Buddhist text from the twelfth century:

Accustom yourself to constantly beholding the mind. When you are proficient in beholding your mind in non-intentional awareness, so that object and mind are not separated from one another, you experience non-dualistic, original consciousness.

During Zazen, Zen meditation, we practise letting the mind dwell in non-intentional awareness. This happens without effort, since true Zen meditation is not a question of doing but rather of pure consciousness. Yet when we notice during meditation that our mind, rather than being collected, is unconcentrated and scattered, it is a great mistake for us to be angry about our thoughts. We must not let any rejection of our thoughts arise. A rejecting attitude to thinking only exhausts us. Therefore we must never try to forcefully suppress thinking.

When waves of thoughts arise during meditation then pay no attention to them. Let the thoughts just float by like passing clouds, without taking any heed of them. Do not start to analyse where they come from and where they are going and do not try to suppress thinking.

For thoughts are activated by our discriminating mind with its tendency to grasp and suppress and only solidify when we take heed of them. In this way, chains of thought are then created, which become autonomous and draw our attention away.

Therefore, do not form any reference to them, simply be the witness – the impartial observer behind all experiences – and nothing else. When you simply perceive the thoughts, without any reference to them in the form of grasping and rejecting, they will not form any chains of thought. The thoughts dissolve of their own accord in the radiating, clear self-awareness of the Mind. That is why the Chinese Zen Master Hui-hai says in the ninth century: When your mind moves do not follow it and it will detach itself from the movement. And when your mind rests on whatever it may be, do not follow it and it will detach itself from that on which it rests.

Zen breathing

Awareness of mind during Zen meditation essentially depends on the right breathing. For body, breath and mind form an inseparable unit. When your breathing is flat and lacks stability, the mind will equally be unstable and thus restless. Yet when your breathing is calm, the mind will also be calm and clear.

Zen breathing is deep, tranquil breathing in which the focus lies in the lower abdomen. In this region, known in Zen as "Hara", we experience a feeling of stability and accumulated energy during Zazen. However, in their attempt to feel their Hara, many people make the mistake of forcefully pressing their breathing downwards, thus causing pressure on their lower abdomen. But this is completely wrong and only leads to mental and physical tension. The prerequisite to tranquil breathing in unison

with body, breath and mind is that we observe our breathing by consciously concentrating on it. The essence of Zen-breathing is to reach a state in our continual practice in which we forget to be aware of the breathing.

Crystal-clear awareness

The fundamental essence of Zen meditation practice is the correct attitude of mind. This is a state of heedfulness, combined with effortlessness and non-intentionality. This means that each intention we have during meditation causes mental tension. There is nothing more to do than to leave the mind as it is naturally. Therefore, during meditation be detached, relaxed and at the same time absolutely aware and heedful. Yet this heedful awareness of mind, which requires no thoughts, does not mean that you control the mind, for that would mean enforcing and is contrary to all Buddhist practice. If we think, "I must hold on to spiritual awareness, I mustn't stray from it in any way and let thoughts arise," then this only leads to increased mental activity. The inevitable result is a state of mental and physical tension, since tension is suppressed desire and suppressed desire always causes tension.

Instead, awareness of mind means that we abide with ourselves in a detached, relaxed attitude, and in serene, cheerful placidity observe our own mind. When we let all arising thoughts come and go, without intervening in any way, they will dissolve of their own accord since they are inherently empty and thus "unreal". This uncontrived state of mind, which neither blocks nor fabricates, is the original, enlightened Heart-Consciousness of all buddhas. Zen Master Lin-chuan says:

Only the intentionless, clear mind perceives itself.

By impartially observing we can see how the mind projects, and how waves of thoughts on the surface of the mind emerge and once again vanish. Yet when we lapse from our awareness, then first of all there are just tiny waves, but these become larger and larger, until finally, we are completely washed away by them. Here, it is useful to know that the mind regains its clarity as soon as it becomes aware that it has lost its attentiveness.

Seeing through the dream

The lucid, effortless, empty self-awareness of the self-radiating One Mind is our true nature. And this is what we must continuously experience; which means not only on the meditation cushion but also in the "midst" of the world, everywhere and at all times.

Even when we lie in bed in the evening we should make it clear to ourselves before we go to sleep that everything we experience in our dreams is just images – everything is empty, everything is just projection. Thereby, you can even use the phenomena of dreams for your spiritual

practice by dissolving the dreams into the void on the path of Tantric transformation. This Tantric practice of dream-yoga leads you to a higher consciousness and deeper understanding of the voidness, and consequently the deceptive nature of all phenomena. In this way, over time you can achieve continuous consciousness, which remains equally in the waking state as during dreaming.

Thus whoever is able to constantly retain the spiritual, lucid consciousness lying at the base of everything, everywhere and in all situations, is truly on the path to liberation. Also at the end of his worldly life of space and time, in the process of dying he will be in awareness of mind.

The moment of dying will then be a great opportunity for him to reach Enlightenment. He will be able to see through the deceptive nature of all phenomena and will rise above the dark mists of phenomena into the clear light of Reality.

8

Moment-Consciousness

Retaining the centre

Your own mind and the boundless expanse of the One Mind are one and the same reality, just like a wave and the ocean. But in order to experience this all-embracing wholeness it is absolutely necessary that you achieve an attitude of mind in which you are no longer trapped in discriminating, conceptual thought, and instead you dwell in awareness of mind.

When we strive to observe our mind we will nevertheless find that we are never really in the present moment. For our consciousness has the habitual tendency of constantly

producing thoughts and occupying itself with the past and the future. In the process, the present moment is only fleetingly perceived. For this reason it happens only very seldom that we devote our entire concentration to what we are currently doing.

Thinking in itself is neither positive nor negative, thoughts come and thoughts go and they have no reality of their own. Yet when we lose our spiritual awareness and our thoughts become autonomous we are under the illusion of past and future, and we have fallen from our centre. It is then fundamentally important that we stop our constantly fabricating mind by totally focussing our attention on "now". Be completely aware of the present moment and thus in awareness of mind. This is the only way we can achieve a state of consciousness of continuous crystal clear self-awareness in all that we do.

Unbound activity

Through this holistic Zen practice we gain the ability to spontaneously adapt to all situations with our whole being and deal with them accordingly, without losing the tranquillity of our awareness in the process. For tranquillity and movement do not mutually exclude one another. On the contrary, they complement each other and as such they must be experienced as a unit. That is why the Chinese Zen Master Hung-ying-ming says in the sixteenth century:

> The stillness in stillness is not real stillness. Only when there is movement in stillness and stillness in movement can the spiritual rhythm appear which pervades heaven and earth.

Therefore always remember this: active participation in the world and silent mindfulness do not obstruct one another and are not incompatible opposites. Only when we discriminate between worldly and spiritual life do we make two out of them. There are so many people who, in their limited dualistic attitude, truly believe that leading a spiritual life means renouncing everything by withdrawing from the "evil world" with its temptations and distractions.

However, a true student of Zen lives completely unattached in the world and is not hindered by anything. In the midst of the demands of our modern life he remains inwardly free and independent of everything.

Since his mind is without discrimination, he is free from grasping and rejecting and does not cling to anything. He does what needs doing and yet does not cling to his actions. Thus he is able to penetrate through to the essence amidst all worldly situations. Since he is inwardly detached from everything, there is no need for him to flee the world as do those who know no better. In the words of Zen Master Huang-po:

> The ignorant one avoids the external world,
> but not the thoughts on the world.
> The wise one does not avoid the external world,
> but he eschews the thoughts on the world.

The wise one lives from out of the all-embracing wholeness of being and by experiencing consubstantiality he recognises that he is one with all beings. This can be seen by his open heart and his compassionate love for all beings. He lives in the midst of the ever-changing world – he comes, goes and acts as the situation requires and is completely free and unattached.

9

The all-embracing wholeness of being

Non-discriminating wisdom

The true man of Zen lives in total freedom. Everywhere, wherever he may be he experiences the glory of Divine Being. In the words of Zen Master Yuan-wu from the twelfth century:

> When you achieve the freedom of Zen nothing ties you and you thoroughly unfold in unity. Then, for you, there are no worldly things beyond Buddhist truth and no Buddhist truth beyond worldly things.

One often hears from proponents of the esoteric scene that Nirvana and Samsara, in other words, the highest truth and the world of birth and death, must be combined with one another. Yet such sayings are utter rubbish and are not compatible with the truth of Zen.

Nirvana and Samsara need not be combined since there is absolutely nothing to combine, for they are one and the same reality. It would be just like saying that the sea and the waves on its surface must be combined. This would make no sense since the sea and the waves are an all-embracing, indivisible oneness, a unique harmonic whole.

In order to understand this, spiritual clear-sightedness is required – a clear, untarnished insight, with which we see things as they really are. For what hampers us in perceiving our original nature is nothing other than the force of habitual, dualistic deception. This is autonomous, discriminating thinking with its accepting and rejecting. It is the discrimination into beautiful and ugly, good and bad, right and wrong.

All this must fall. And then we will see that Sukhavati Paradise – the paradise of boundless light – is present in its entire splendour because it has always been present. Then we will realise that Sukhavati Paradise is not an otherworldly dimension but – "the original state of consciousness of our true being".

Each moment, this reality of Divine Being is before us it its complete perfection – nothing exists beyond it. It is omnipresent, silent and pure and manifests itself as wonderful, mysterious, peaceful joy.

Liberation

We come from nowhere, and since there is neither space nor time, there is also nowhere we could go. There is nothing to achieve, for everything is an all-encompassing whole which contains everything within it.

Whoever fails to recognise this begins to brood and discriminate. Next he starts to whine and complain and says, "I feel like I'm making no progress on the spiritual path. Whatever could be the cause of this?" The answer is as simple as it is clear. It is because he is projecting, and these projections between him and absolute reality become "stencils" through which he views the world.

Everything now takes on exactly those distortions and forms which he sees through his self-projected stencils. Thus, he looks through his stencils onto the boundless expanse of being and sees only his own limited forms, and then thinks, completely convinced: So this is the truth, this is reality. Yet Zen says:

Throw everything away, whatever it may be!

Only thus can you attain liberation and escape your self-made limitations. "Liberation" is the principal word in Zen Buddhism. In Zen it all comes down to inner spiritual liberation. The Chinese Zen Master Huang-po likewise says:

> The mind is filled with radiant clarity so cast away the darkness of your old, dead concepts. Free yourselves of everything!

Truly having the courage to free yourself of everything, whatever it may be, is the way to Enlightenment. Even the smallest obstacle must be removed because the biggest is equal to the smallest and the smallest is equal to the biggest. A koan from the Mumonkan, a Chinese collection of Zen sayings from the thirteenth century, beyond the capacity of logical thinking, tells us this too. It goes as follows:

> A cow goes through a window. Its head, its horns, its stomach and its four legs are already through. But how can it be that its tail does not go through?

To make this very clear: the light of the One Mind shines forth only when everything that is blocking the light, however small it is or beautiful and sacred, has been swept out of the way. Zen Master Lin Chi from the ninth century puts it in this powerful way:

Clear every obstacle from the path.
If you meet Buddha, then kill Buddha!
Only thus will you obtain deliverance,
only thus will you escape the chains and become free.

10

Cloudless clarity

Clearing the mind

Zen practice is about clarifying the mind so that we experience its original, cloudless clarity. So what is this veil which darkens the radiating clarity of the mind? It is all our deep-rooted thought habits and behavioural patterns. It is all the interwoven memories of our dead past with which we generally identify ourselves.

We believe that all this belongs to our personality to the point where we are convinced we are the sum of these experiences and memories. And what is more, we even project these conditionings onto everything. We believe "this is the world and those are the others", for we are indeed incapable of seeing things differently due to our stencil of dualistic perspective.

Unfortunately, most people cling tightly to this conditioned perspective and only act out their mindless routine within their self-created boundaries. As a result, they deem impossible everything that goes beyond their limited powers of imagination. In this way, they constantly project an accumulation of dark clouds of discriminating, conceptual thinking which obscure the boundless expanse of the Mind and thus obscure their own divine being. Zen Master Yuan-wu from the twelfth century therefore says:

> When enlightened Zen masters provide teachings for the spiritual path, their only concern is to clarify the mind so it arrives at its source.

But how should we clarify the mind in order to achieve the right perspective and experience our true being? The Buddhist teachings say: "The mind is clarified when we penetrate the illusionary nature of all phenomena and liberate ourselves from all our confusion by achieving spiritual lucidity." Here it is important for us to realise that everything to which we attach such infinite importance and meaning has no real existence – no Beingness of itself.

The original purity of the mind

Buddhists therefore characterise this illusionary and dream-like nature of all phenomena as "voidness" – Sunyata. In the Lankavatara Sutra, one of the most important sacred texts of Mahayana Buddhism from the fifth century, we read:

Perceptions appear real to the mind, agitated by its habitual tendencies. Yet they do not really exist – they are empty and are themselves only Mind. It is wrong to view them as external reality.

Therefore, when Zen masters give instruction it is always their sole intention to clarify the student's mind so that he experiences the purity of his original mind. In the language of Zen, this pure, empty mind is "our original, true face before our birth". It is like the sun, which shines bright and clear in a radiating blue sky, unmoved and unchanging. Amidst all our daily activities the mind lights up everything and shines forth from all things.

This primal birthless and deathless reality, lying at the base of all being, is constantly present and the basis of all our experiences, even if we do not consciously perceive it. It is not that it is sometimes more and sometimes less present. No; it remains unchangingly present – it is just that we are not really present.

However, if we would turn our whole spiritual energy inwards, which we constantly disperse and squander by pointlessly brooding over all sorts of things the whole time, we could experience this reality as our true self. Huang-po therefore says:

> If you could only make yourselves free from your discriminating thinking, you would achieve everything.

So liberate yourself from your habitual distractions and conditioned perspective of discriminating, conceptual thinking. Immerse yourself with your whole being – body, breath and mind – in "Now, the present moment".

Not missing out on the essential

Stop analysing why this or that is so or not so, or whether it was so or not so. The folly of analysing everything is illustrated in the old Buddhist parable of the farmer and the burning house:

A farmer who returns from his work in the field sees that his house is on fire. All of the villagers have rushed to help put out the fire.

But the farmer calls, "Wait, stop, not so fast. First of all, I want to know how the fire started and if someone set fire to the house! If so, what did he look like? Was he male or female? Was he big or small? Was his hair black or brown? Did he have a beard or not? Was he old or was he young? Did he come on foot, or did he ride a donkey or an ox?"

The farmer goes on and on – and in the meantime his house has burned to the ground.

If we are not truly present, and instead, our mind is scattered here and there, we miss the essence of the present moment. If we do not consciously live in Here and Now, we will never attain the experience of our true being. And so we will sway back and forth for many incarnations from one rebirth to the next and eke out a pitiful existence in the "shadowy darkness of Maya".

However, this shadowy darkness of Maya is nothing other than projections, brought forth by our spiritual blindness, which have become autonomous. These projections are all of our well-worn behaviour-patterns, hypotheses, memories and fears, all our pseudo-concerns in this apparent multitudinous world. We take all of this to be true life. We take the spectacle of birth and death on the stage of life to be real and cling to it in fear. Yet Zen calls to us:

Let go of everything; for the Mind is filled with radiant clarity. Free yourself of everything, whatever it may be!

11

The Path to immortality

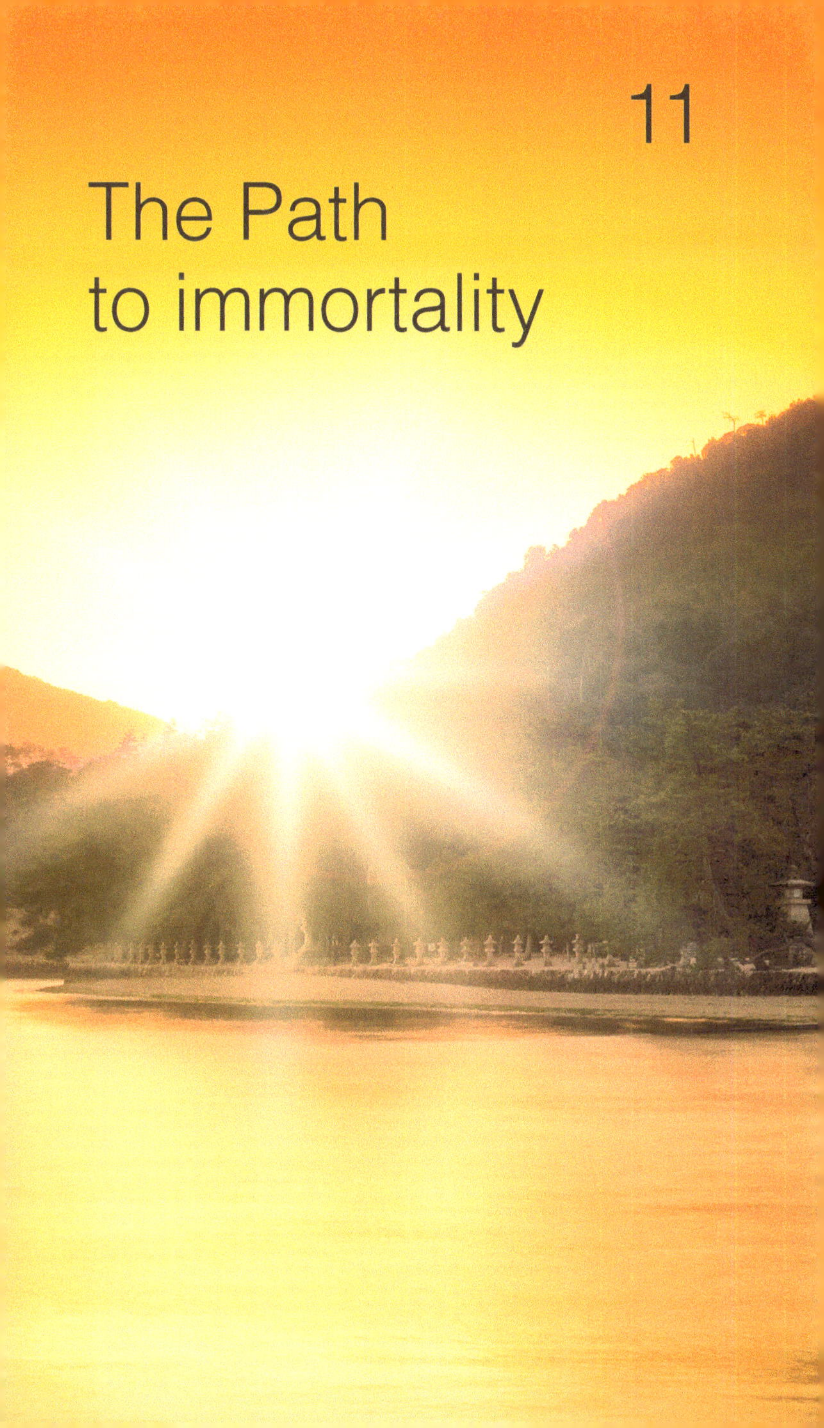

The cheerfulness of the mind

Natural cheerfulness, as the cheerful, serene reflection of the mind, is the original state of our true being. Thus, all conditioned notions of the earnestness of the spiritual path are in the eyes of Zen nothing more than empty concepts and must be transcended. They just create obstacles which restrict us. They only chain our mind and must finally be dropped if we wish to attain this cheerful, serene reflection of the mind. For this reason, the Tibetan Mahamudra Master Buton says in the fourteenth century:

> Silent, cheerfulness of the mind is a means of realising the truth, for in order to come to this realisation, the confused, restless mind must become pure and cheerful.

When the weather is cheerful, no dark clouds hang in the sky. Cheerful means light and clear. Light and clear means the completely natural, original condition of our birthless and deathless mind. Yet, only when we completely immerse ourselves in this natural state will we be able to experience the splendour of our true being. However, you cannot achieve this by viewing everyday life in the world as a hindrance on the spiritual path, and thereby living in a deadened state of sense and mind. Whoever negates life this way and goes around like a living corpse in indifferent ignorance certainly dares not hope to enter the great, eternal life at the moment of his death. That would be a big mistake.

It is indeed most astonishing that of all people, those who do not truly live during this life are the ones who yearn most for an eternal life. Whoever is already dead here in this world will also be so in the transcendent world. He cannot hope for an eternal, blissful life. If we want eternal life, we must truly live "now" and completely immerse ourselves "now-here" in Beingness, in true life.

A meaningful life

Only those who "truly" live this life will be transformed at the moment of death into the great life – into immortality. And in response to the age-old question of man: "Is there life after death or not?", the correct reply in the spirit of Zen is: "Is there true life 'before' death?" That is the crucial question.

If we wish to experience true life here, it is absolutely necessary to have boundless trust in the reality of our true being. This trust is an unswerving belief in the original purity of our own birthless and deathless mind. From this a great force grows within us which more and more enables us to achieve uninterrupted awareness of mind. Thereby we become able to experience the preciousness of each moment with our whole being, and live crystal clear awareness and active partaking in life as a single reality.

Then real life reveals itself to us and our life becomes a true life, filled with meaning. Everywhere, wherever it may be, we will increasingly experience the omnipresent reality of our true being. It is just like early in the morning when the sun rises on the horizon: firstly it is still dark, yet then it slowly begins to turn lighter and lighter, until the sun is high in the sky and illuminates the whole landscape in its light.

The Chinese Zen Master Yuan-wu from the twelfth century gives us a very striking description of this wonderful state of consciousness:

Your existence is free of all boundaries; you have become open, light, and transparent. You gain an enlightening view into the true nature of all things, which now appear to you as a mass of glowing fairy-tale flowers without any tangible reality.

This is where your true self, the original countenance of your true being, reveals itself. This is where the wonderful landscape of your true native land lies unveiled before you.

Glossary

Amitabha Sanskrit, "Boundless light", Jap. "Amida". One of the most important buddhas in Mahayana Buddhism. It is the buddha of "western paradise" Sukhavati, which is not linked to a particular location but instead means a state of consciousness of boundless light, of love and comprehension.

According to the teachings of Shin-Buddhism, anyone who in deep faith calls Amitabha's name (especially at the hour of death), will be reborn in Sukhavati paradise. In the "Pure Land school", this invocation is known as Namu Amida Butsu, "worship of the buddha Amitabha".

Hara Jap., literally: "Belly, abdomen". This common →Zen term signifies the area approximately three finger widths below the belly button as the centre of all being. It is the centre of every person and at the same time the centre of the universe. Through the practice of zazen and correct breathing a great energy and power develop in this centre. Hara, as the centre of energy, is in Zen the point of origin of all activity (as in the meaning of "acting on intuition", but in Zen its meaning goes much deeper).

Karma Sanskrit, literally: "Action or deed". The law of cause and effect, by which all thoughts and actions have a corresponding consequence. Through this we determine the quality of our own lives and influence that of others.

Mushin Jap., (Chin. Wu-hsin); "Non-thinking, non-consciousness, seclusion of the mind". A natural state of mind entirely without aim, beyond all thought. Mushin and Munen (Chin. Wu-nien) together form one of the central concepts of Zen. In Zen, Mushin does not mean ignorance or spiritual stupor but rather that the mind is so steadfast within itself that is cannot be perturbed by external circumstances, no matter what they may be. It means that the mind remains clear and free and dwells on nothing, not even on the thought of non-thinking.

Samsara Sanskrit, literally: "roaming". The cycle of birth and death. The aim of all Buddhists and Hinduists is liberation from samsara, and thus from suffering. It is liberation from the imprisonment in the wheel of birth, ageing, despair, illness, pain and death.

Satori Jap. (Chin. Wu). Zen term for the experience of Enlightenment, or awakening. Satori is far more than an intuitive understanding of true Being, as in the experience of Kensho, since the person who experiences Satori dissolves entirely into it. In →Zen, Satori is described as the rebirth of the true Self once the false, illusory self; the ego-delusion has died the "Great Death".

Shunyata Sanskrit (Jap. Ku), literally: "emptiness, void". According to the teachings of Mahayana nothing possesses an autonomous, lasting substance. All things are empty and thus without self-nature. The Shunyata teaching is one of the cornerstones of the whole of Mahayana Buddhism and accordingly of →Zen. It is very subtle and cannot be expressed in words. Although there is extensive literature covering this subject, Shunyata can only be completely understood by those who have experienced it themselves in the experience of Enlightenment (→Satori).

Taoism There are two main streams of Taoism – the philosophical stream: Tao-chia, and the religious stream: Tao-chiao. Tao-chia dates back to the Taoist master Lao-tse and his book, the Tao Te King. Here, acting without intent in unison with the Tao is seen as the highest ideal. On the other hand, the aim of the religious Taoism is physical immortality. It is to be achieved through breathing exercises, physical exercises and certain sexual practices.

Wu-wei Chin., literally: "Non-action" in the sense of "action without intention". However, this Taoist term is not to be confused with passively doing nothing. Much rather, it means the attitude of mind of non-intervention in the natural course of things. In truth, Wu-wei is a highly effective state of mind, in which any action is possible at any time. By living non-action, the Taoist sage is in unison with Tao, whose universal power is brought to bear exactly due to this non-action. The great Taoist master of old, Lao-tse thus says in his → Tao Te King: Tao is eternally without action, but nothing remains undone.

Wu-Wei is therefore a matter of creative non-action, an actless conduct which underlies the mental attitude of non-intervention and the courage of letting things happen. Wu-Wei transcends both extremes – restless activity and absolute inactivity. It is a non-action of the unimportant, which at the same time allows the essential to take effect.

Zen Jap., an abbreviation of "Zenna", the Japanese way of reading the Chinese "channa" (in short, chan), which itself is a transcript of the Sanskrit word "Dhyana". Zen-Buddhism developed in the 6th and 7th centuries in China from the combination of Bodhidarma's transmission of Indian Dhyana-Buddhism and Chinese →Taoism. Characteristic of Zen is its particularly strong emphasis on the experience of Enlightenment (→Satori). Integral to Zen is also the development of intuitive comprehension through meditation rather than through intellectual studies. The fundamental characteristics of Zen were summarized in the early Tang-Dynasty in four short statements in Chinese:

1. Transmission outside the orthodox teachings
2. Independence from holy scriptures
3. Directly pointing to the heart-mind
4. Insight into one's own nature and attainment of Buddhahood

Contact

ZEN CENTER
TAO 道禪 CHAN

Tao Chan Zentrum e.V.
65195 Wiesbaden
Germany

The Tao- Chan Zen Centre is under the personal direction of Zen Master Zensho W. Kopp.
During his many years as an active spiritual master, a large community of students have come together whom he regularly instructs.

Zen-Day
Twice a month, the Tao-Chan Zen Centre organises an open Zen-day, led by Zen Master Zensho W. Kopp.

Information and registration
Tel. +49 (0)611 940 623-1 Fax -2
www.tao-chan.org
www.facebook.com/ZenZentrumTaoChan

ZENSHO W. KOPP

AWAKENING
TO YOUR TRUE
SELF

THE ZEN WAY
OF ALL-EMBRACING MYSTICISM

Awaking to your true Self
The ZEN way of all-embracing mysticism
ISBN 978-3-744895-38-5

Books by Zensho W. Kopp

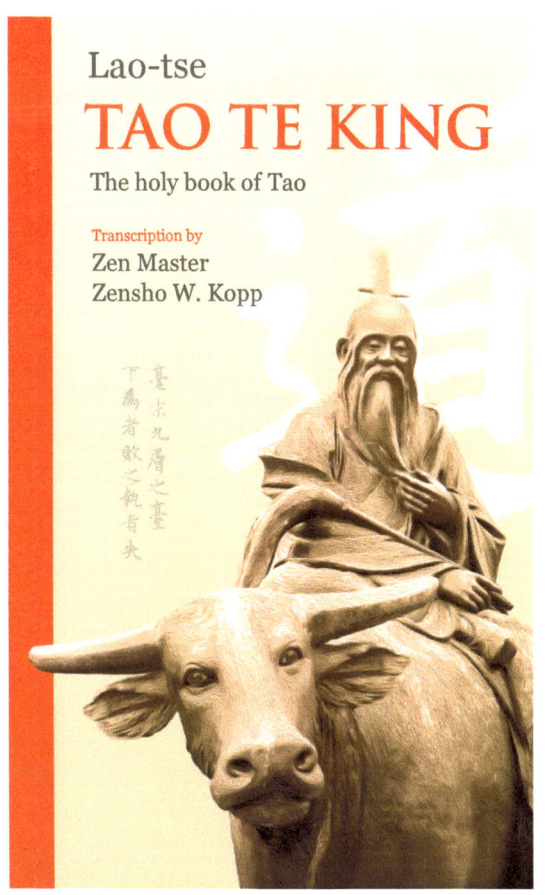

Lao-tse
TAO TE KING
The holy book of Tao

Transcription by
Zen Master
Zensho W. Kopp

Lao-tse – Tao Te King
The holy book of Tao

Transcription by
Zen Zensho W. Kopp

ISBN 978-3-744895-38-5

Books by Zensho W. Kopp

Mysterious revelations of the Eternal
Warecolours and sayings of a western Zen Master

ISBN 978-3-744895-96-5

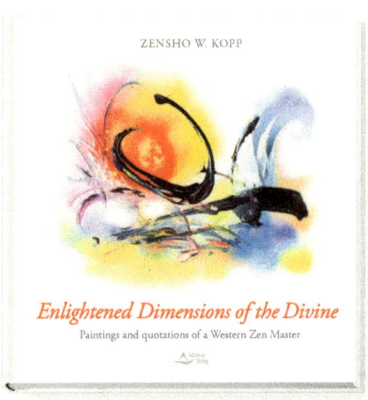

Enlightened Dimensions of the Divine
Paintings and quotations of a Western Zen Master

ISBN 978-1-4827-9942-2

Books by Zensho W. Kopp

Words of the Awakened Mind
Aphorisms of a Western Zen Master

ISBN 978-3-8482-4134-7

The Freedom of Zen
The Zen book that shatters all limits and bounds

ISBN 978-3-8391-6893-6

FSC
www.fsc.org

MIX

Papier aus ver-
antwortungsvollen
Quellen
Paper from
responsible sources

FSC® C105338